FIGHT THE POWER – Public Enemy

Now tell me Lovey. Why is it when we as Black People stand up for our rights, we are racist?

Deemed as troublemakers.

Some are muzzled.

Killed – assassinated by the enemies that fear us and what we can do because; we are enlightening the minds of our people to get out of their racist, unfair, and unbalanced systems that use the Black Race for profit and as; Guinea Pigs and Scapegoats to suit their unjust needs and wants; greed.

When we talk about oppression and racism we are cast as troublemakers.

Are the enemies of those who profit off Slavery – the Mental and Systemic Slavery they have us bound; chained in.

Now Lovey, didn't Public Enemy tell us:

"OUR FREEDOM OF SPEECH IS FREEDOM OF DEATH."

1

Now tell me; *"WHICH BLACK PERSON IS FREE TO LIVE GOOD AND TRUE IN THE UNITED STATES OF DEATH - AMERICA?"*

Are Black People not used as their game?
Are Black People not their prey - hunted?

Are Blacks not the ones to be eradicated - killed by Whites, and yes, our own?

So now tell me. *"WHAT DEATH CAN BRING ABOUT FREEDOM?"*

When we tell our Black People to change their way of thinking and doing things as well as, come out of White Societies of Slavery *WE ARE SEEN AS EVIL - THE ENEMY OF THE STATE, AND THE EVIL SYSTEMS THAT KEEP BLACKS OPPRESSED AND CHAINED TO THEIR UNJUST AND UNBALANCED SYSTEMS OF LIES AND DECEIT.*

When I look at some of our own Blacks based on hue, I have to wonder about them because; many has and have been brainwashed; conditioned to be White, Think White, Live White, Praise White, Praise their White Gods, and more. Therefore, they will not see the need to change and get out of Babylon - Hell.

NO WHITE GOD - Sizzla

Now tell me, <u>CAN THE WHITE RACE AND THEIR GOD SAVE BLACK PEOPLE WHEN ALL THE WHITE RACE AND THEIR GOD DO IS OPPRESS AND KEEP BLACKS BOUND TO THEIR LIES AND DECEIT; ALL THAT IS UNCLEAN?</u>

Now tell me, <u>IS THERE ONE GOD ALONE?</u>

Do the different races not have their own god based on Black Doctrines?

Now tell me Lovey, how can we be aware when we as Blacks refuse to open our eyes and see clearly.

Yes, fight the power but; our power should be leaving out of the systems that betray us, and use us not just as slaves but; their Guinea Pigs and Scapegoats.

Lovey we have knowledge and buying power but, instead of utilizing our buying power and knowledge the right way, we do not; why?

Many things I cannot comprehend with us as Black People. We complain about so much yet, in all we complain about; <u>WE ARE NOT EFFECTIVE IN HELPING OURSELVES AND LEAVING OUT OF COUNTRIES THAT OPPRESS US; WHY?</u>

<u>CHANGES</u> – Tupac

Are we that ignorant Lovey?

I know _MARCHING_ truly do now work.

When we March, we are saying we want to stay in oppressive societies that oppress us, cage us, muzzle us, and kill us.

Now Lovey, when are we as Blacks going to learn that; _WHEN WE AS BLACKS TRY TO EDUCATE OUR OWN BLACK PEOPLE WE BECOME THE ENEMY OF DEATH AND THEIR PEOPLE?_

Blacks are not supposed to know the truth. Therefore, the truth is kept from us.

WHEN WE AS BLACK PEOPLE KNOW THE TRUTH AND FULL TRUTH OF US, WE WILL TRULY FIND OUT WE DO NOT NEED THE WHITE RACE – ANY RACE FOR THAT MATTER.

WHEN ARE WE AS BLACK PEOPLE GOING TO REALIZE, IT'S BEST TO LEAVE OUT OF OPPRESSIVE LANDS?

No Lovey, we can build Black – Black People good and true. But in truth, _how many Blacks want this?_

We say support Black Business, but are we truly doing this?

Are we as Black People truly helping each other?

4

Those that can afford it, are they truly helping their Black Own?

There is so much that we can do for self yet, we are not breaking away from our conditioned way of thinking and doing things; why?

Many lands do not want or need us in them so, _why can't we build our own lands?_

Why do we have to be like _CAGED BIRDS_ in the different lands that oppress and supress us including, muzzle us?

WHY ARE WE AS A PEOPLE LIVING IN GLOBAL ABUSE?

Do we love abuse so much that we will stay in it Lovey?

DON'T LOOK BACK – Peter Tosh

Lovey, we as Black People do not have to live in _GLASS HOUSES._ We can live free but, _how many want to leave out of White Society, and break away from White Rule?_

Lovey _EXODUS._

Why can't we leave out of the places that truly hate us, and build us without looking back at the lands that OPPRESS BLACK PEOPLE.

Lovey, <u>THEY DON'T LIKE US, THEN; DON'T WANT OR NEED OUR MONEY, RESOURCES, MEN, WOMEN, KIDS, LAND, FOOD, GOD, BOOKS, CREATION, KNOWLEDGE, RHYTHM, VIBE, VIBRATION, AND MORE COME ON NOW.</u>

No Lovey. Do you truly think I would feed my enemies once I leave out of Oppressive Lands?

I truly don't need oppression Lovey come on now.

Once I move away, there is absolutely no coming back for me you know this Lovey come on now.

Why do you think I bug you so much for land space, a house, a country that I can live true and free in?

Why should I live in Oppressive Lands and be miserable all my life?

You did not put me on this Earth to be used and abused by anyone.

You did not put me on this Earth to be hated by anyone.

You did not put me on Earth to build my enemies come on now.

You did not put me on Earth to be controlled by anyone come on now.

You don't like me, I am not staying around you nor; am I supporting you Financially.

<u>Why should I give you my blessing by supporting your economy?</u>

Why should I build you and take away from my Black Own once I leave out of your oppressive systems of injustice and hatred?

No Lovey. It is us as Blacks that are the foolish ones that; <u>REFUSE TO LEAVE OUT OF LANDS THAT TRULY DON'T LIKE US.</u>

Now let me ask you this Lovey. *When did you say, Black People stay in the lands of your enemies and let them continually use and abuse you?*

When did you Lovey tell Black People or anyone to go into unclean lands?

When did you Lovey tell Black People or anyone to go into the land and lands of their enemies?

<u>So, why are we as Blacks not holding our own, and building our own good and true?</u>

Why are we as Black People living careless?

Why are we fighting to stay in Oppressive Lands?

<u>Absolutely no one can or will get Justice in Unjust Lands.</u>

When are we as a Race and People going to wake up and see as well as, know; "*EVIL CANNOT BE JUST AND NEVER WILL BE JUST?*"

No Lovey. *WHY CAN'T WE AS BLACK PEOPLE TAKE A PAGE OUT OF YOUR BOOK AND, MOVE AWAY FROM ALL UNCLEAN PEOPLE AND THINGS?*

Come on Lovey. *DID YOU NOT SEPARATE YOURSELF FROM MOTHER EARTH?*

Come on Lovey. Are you not happy you are not in Earth?

Are you not happy you are not on/in Earth living amongst the unclean?

Sorry Mother Earth truly do not be offended. Humans dirtied you, and Lovey left out of you. Why can't we as Black People and You Mother Earth learn from Lovey and, move away from all who oppress us, dirty us, abuse us, use us, kill us, and more.

You Mother Earth can walk – truly walk away from humans by taking your goodness from wicked and evil lands yet, you refuse to in my view; why?

You are literally dying Mother Earth now tell me, ARE HUMANS WORTH DYING FOR?

<u>IS YOUR LIFE THAT WORTHLESS AND VALUELESS TO YOU THAT YOU WOULD DIE – COMMIT SUICIDE FOR HUMANS?</u>

Now, if so being the case Mother Earth, why did God create you – let you be born?

So basically, <u>**YOU ARE BLACK JESUS THEN.**</u> You are the one to lay your life down for wicked and evil people knowing that evil destroy and kill, and evil cannot be saved.

What were you truly hoping for in humans Mother Earth?

What were you thinking when it came to your life?

Did you think Lovey would concede and save all who are wicked and evil?

Did you not think Lovey would leave you to your choice of housing Death, and the Children and People of Death?

Now tell me Mother Earth. You know unclean make all who are clean dirty. So, why continue to dirty you in this way?

Do you not see how I complain to Lovey about cleanliness even, moving away from some of my children?

Mother Earth, you see the mess I have to live in. Just look how messy my daughter is. Well, the mess she purposely leaves around her common area for me to be upset.

<u>Listen, YOU CANNOT DIE FOR LIFE NO ONE CAN.</u> In order to attain Life, you have to live good and true. <u>So, why are you sacrificing yourself for Humans and Death?</u>

<u>WHAT ARE YOU GUILTY OF MOTHER EARTH?</u>

Now tell me Mother Earth. <u>Are you that naïve to think humans would save you?</u>

Are humans not the ones that are destroying you?

So, why put your trust and truth in humans come on now?

<u>GUILTINESS</u> – Bob Marley

Now let me ask you this Mother Earth.

<u>Are you not a victim when it comes to humans and life here on Earth?</u>

You are the one eating the bread of sorrow because, you are allowing evil to devour and kill you.

Now tell me. Do humans truly care about you?

<u>IS YOUR LIFE OF ANY IMPORTANCE TO HUMANS HERE ON EARTH?</u>

Blacks are oppressed and, it is us that cannot wake up therefore; Blacks live in vain, die in vain, sin reckless and rude, <u>are the ones eating the BREAD OF SAD TOMORROW BECAUSE, WE REFUSE TO UTILIZE OUR GOODNESS AND TRUTH POSITIVELY TO HELP US.</u>

You Mother Earth cannot continue to do the same as Black People because, <u>ABSOLUTELY NO ONE CAN FIND GOODNESS IN EVIL</u> come on now.

<u>ONE DROP</u> – Bob Marley

<u>STOP THE CORRUPTION</u> – Admiral Tibet

As Black People we need to find a better way for us to live. We can no longer govern ourselves under Colonial Rule.

We have to get rid of the conditioning we've been brainwashed in come on now.

It's time for us to live Black and get back to our good and true roots come on now.

<u>It's time we stop forgiving those who abuse us because, when we forgive our enemies;</u>

they cannot, and will not face hell for the injustice they've done onto us come on now.

Why the hell should our enemies get away for their unfair, and unjust treatment of us?

They hurt us yet, get away with it because; they teach FORGIVENESS OF SIN WITHOUT YOU KNOWING THAT; WHEN THEY MASSACRE YOU RECKLESS AND RUDE, RAPE AND ABUSE YOU RECKLESS AND RUDE, KILL YOU RECKLESS AND RUDE, LIE ON YOU RECKLESS AND RUDE, AND YOU FORGIVE THEM; YOUR ENEMIES, THEY DO NOT FACE HELL FOR ALL THE ILLS THEY'VE DONE ONTO YOU.

THEY GO SCOTT FREE BECAUSE YOU LET THEM GO. THEREFORE, THEY SPEND NO TIME IN HELL FOR THEIR SINS. SO, now tell me; WHO ARE THE FOOLS?

It is certainly not your enemy, it's you because; you forgave them of their ills; wrongs they've done unto you.

Therefore, it's time for us to stop letting other batta bruise wi. It's time we stop forgiving our enemies.

It's time for us to live so that we can move forward in life.

It's time we truly educate ourselves with the truth.

It's time we truly turn back to the cleanliness of our Black God.

It's time for us to live right.
Talk right.
Be right.
Be clean.
Talk clean.
Think clean, and more.

Now. LOOK AT BLACK HISTORY.

WHY ARE WE ALLOWING WHITE PEOPLE TO WRITE OUR HISTORY FOR US?

WHY ARE WE AS BLACK PEOPLE ALLOWING WHITE PEOPLE TO LIE ON US HISTORICALLY, LIFE WISE, GOD WISE, KNOWLEDGE WISE, EDUCATIONALLY, JUDICIALLY, HEALTH WISE, FOOD WISE, ECONOMICALLY, PSYCHOLOGICALLY, SOCIALLY, RELIGIOUSLY, POLITICALLY, ENTERTAINMENT WISE, MUSICALLY, AND MORE?

Lovey, Bob Marley tried and died – was murdered because he was using songs to educate his Black Own but like fools, we as Blacks helped to assassinate him. Until this day, *BLACKS STILL DO NOT GET THE MESSAGE OR KNOW THE MESSAGE.* Therefore, we continue fighting each other, sell the devils agenda, accept lies and deceit when it comes to us, live as the scorned, used and abused; chained fools that cannot unite and let the truth set us free from the chains of Death, and Hell that Shackle and Chain us.

Marcus Mosiah Garvey tried, and his own Blacks set him up because; Enterprise was, and still is not important to Blacks. Therefore, we fight down those Blacks that work clean and true to elevate themselves in a good and true way.

We complain about the Chinese and Europeans excelling and taking over yet, what are we as a Race and People doing right collectively to support and elevate *OUR BLACK ECONOMY AND BUSINESSES?*

Instead, we sell out Black Lands and wonder why Blacks Globally are so damn poor when; God gave us all the riches Physically and Spiritually to keep us, maintain us, sustain us, and more. So now tell me, *HOW CAN GOD STAY WITH US AS BLACK PEOPLE – A RACE AND PEOPLE WHEN WE DIVIDE SELF, AND SELL OUT EVERYTHING GOD HAS AND HAVE GIVEN US TO MAKE OUR LIFE EASIER AND WORTH IT?*

Tupac died. But Listen to Changes. He did tell us, we as Black People need to change the way we think, eat, do things, yet, as Blacks; we are still not listening. *Instead of taking up the gun and drugs, change you. Put the crime and violence down and build you positive and good.*

"Take the evil out the people and they be acting right."

Evil can never change. Evil have to be evil. It is you the person that must change you. *As Blacks without RIGHT AND TRUE KNOWLEDGE, WE WILL FOREVER BE SHACKLED AND CHAINED TO DEATH.*

As Blacks we need the true truth of us.

As Blacks we cannot rely on Africa to tell us the truth because they are not.

As Blacks we need to know that not all of Africa is of God.

SO, AS AFRICA CANNOT DEFEND THEIR BLACK GOD, AFRICA CANNOT AND WILL NOT DEFEND YOU THE BLACKS IN THE WEST.

Black Africans defend lies thus, RELIGION, CORRUPTION, AND VOODOO IS PREVELANT ON THE CONTINENT OF AFRICA.

None can tell you, *WHEN WE AS BLACK PEOPLE WALK AWAY FROM OUR BLACK GOD, THE DIVORCE – WALKING AWAY IS INDEFINITE.*

So

BLACK TRUTH IS A CURSE ONTO THOSE WHO HATE US – WHITES, AND SOME OF OUR BLACK OWN.

BLACK TRUTH IS DEATH FOR THOSE BLACKS WHO SPEAK IT – TRY TO EDUCATE, AND TEACH THEIR BLACK OWN. Because, some Blacks do not want to know the truth. The lies and offerings of Sin suit them just fine. So, they pretend they are with you and behind your back, they are crucifying you. Two faced are they thus, many will defend the lies they believe in. Listen, BLACK LIFE IS NOT WHITE LIFE.

BLACK DEATH IS NOT WHITE DEATH IN THAT WAY.

For our enemies, we as Blacks should not live true. We should live enslaved, broken, and beneath them.

So now tell me Black People. AS A RACE AND PEOPLE, WHAT DO WE NEED AND WANT FOR OURSELF?

WHAT CHANGES WOULD YOU LIKE TO SEE FOR YOU GLOBALLY WHEN IT COMES TO LIFE ALL AROUND?

As Blacks, we have to learn to make ourselves satisfied. We cannot want what our oppressors have.

We have to start teaching our children right.

We have to start teaching our children the full and true truth of the Black Race and our Civilization.

We have to find our Black God again and set us free all around.

We have to find our Black God again so that we can live as well as, attain true life once again.

As Blacks, __we cannot live White because; White is not us.__ We are Black therefore, we have to be proud of us and what we as Black People have and has accomplished over the years and centuries.

As Blacks, we __TRULY NEED TO GET BACK OUR TRUE SPIRITUAL SELF.__

As Blacks, we cannot continue to live as the conquered and uneducated come on now.

__Black Economy is not White Economy__ and should never ever be White Economy. Thus, we need to stand for truth. Yes, many in Black Lands are corrupt therefore, it is wise to vote these people out of office good and true.

Corrupt businesses; strive not to buy from the unclean and corrupt.

Yes, I give songs in these books and, not all the artists are clean. I worry not about the *"SOUL OF UNCLEAN ARTISTS."* As long as you get the message I am trying to teach you in a clean and true way then; I am saved, and you are saved. Yes, have shed some of your Sins because, <u>you get the CLEAN MESSAGE I am delivering.</u>

It's not the artists in these books. <u>*"IT'S THE MESSAGE OF CLEANLINESS, WISDOM, AND TRUTH THAT I AM DELIVERING TO YOU."*</u>

So, receive your good and true blessings from, "me and God; Lovey including, Mother Earth."

<u>*Listen, WE CAN NO LONGER LET THE SINS OF OUR BLACK CORRUPT LEADERS FALL ON US; YOU THAT IS IN LANDS RUN BY CORRUPT BLACK LEADERS.*</u> *These leaders have no place to go other than Hell. Truly do not take on their sins and go to hell with them. Your life is worth it. Therefore, do all the good you can to protect your life.*

Now many of you cannot see this but I can.

Take a look at the new <u>*GATEWAY TO HELL*</u> in Iceland. In many ways God and Earth is showing you what many of you will; must face in Hell if you have more Sin than Good. Now, if you think that Lava is Hell like I know it's Hell then, you truly don't know hell because; the fire that burn your spirit is infinitely hotter than the Lava you see spuing and flowing.

Think because, _24 000 Earth Years equal 1 Spiritual Day._ Now tell me, when you tabulate your Sins how will you fair in Hell?

Now reverse it. 24 000 Spiritual Years = 1 Earth Day.

No one can or will escape Hell.

Just as you see the Volcano; this is Hell for some. Now, take away the water that the Lava flow into because, _HELL HATH NO WATER OR AIR CONDITIONERS._ So, tell me, is this what you want for self as Black People?

White People hath not to worry. HELL IS THEIR HOME. GOD DID LOCK THEM OUT OF LIFE THEREFORE, THEY CANNOT SEE GOD OR RESIDE IN THE REALM OF GOD. There is no saving grace for the White Race because, the damage is done. Now; it's your turn Black People.

THE MORE WE LIVE IN LIES, BELIEVE IN LIES, TELL LIES IS, THE FURTHER GOD MOVE AWAY FROM US.

The bible that billions believe in to be the truth of God they too are locked out of Life – the Life of God.

EVERY FACET OF RELIGION IS LOCKED OFF FROM GOD. GOD DO NOT DEAL IN RELIGION BECAUSE RELIGION IS A LIE; UNCLEAN.

Religion is of Death. Therefore, billions bow down to Death.

"GOD CANNOT GO BACK ON HIS OR HER WORD."

"GOD CANNOT SIN."

"LIFE – GOD CANNOT KILL."
"LIFE – GOD CANNOT STEAL."

"CREATION IS NOT PRO-CREATION; NASTY."

"GOD IS CLEAN."

Therefore, humans cast God in their nasty bracket. Thus, the God humans praise and worship is as nasty as them; humans.

Know the evil we believe in destroy us and, take us from life.

Further know. *If you have no savings with God, God cannot save you and, I've told you this in other books.*

You cannot want to be saved and, take yourself from life.

You cannot want to be saved and, God truly do not know you.

You cannot want to be saved and, not have a Chequing, and Savings Account with God.

You cannot want to be saved and, have no Investments in Life – God.

You cannot want to be saved and, do nothing to save yourself with God.

If you know not how to live, how can God save you?
If you have not truth, how can you say you know God?
If you have not truth, how can God know you?

If you cannot speak the truth, how can you speak truth over yourself and others?

If you cannot speak the truth, how can you go to God for saving?

You cannot believe in Death and do all for Death and think the True and Living God is going to save you.

Yes, I know many in the Black Community have and has sold their soul for Money. But I worry not about these people because, *they have to live by the Code of Death.* There is no saving them I know this for a fact without doubt. Thus, many do use their butt and vagina as their breakfast, lunch, and dinner table.

Many women – Black Women and their Children are passed around like Merry-Go-Rounds.

The Code of Death is Sin, and the more you Sin, is the longer you burn Spiritually in Hell. Thus, THE FLESH OF MAN CANNOT TASTE HELL. IT IS YOUR SPIRIT THAT MUST FACE HELL.

So, as Black People, we have to do all now to save ourselves because; the truth has and have been hidden from the lots of you. Many things you truly do not know therefore if you can, *GO TO GOD FOR THE TRUTH.*

Black People are not poor. We are the ones to make ourselves poor. And don't you dare say, take a look at the ghettos some of us live in.

Who created the ghetto?

Who turned the area they are living in into ghettos?

Did God put you in the ghetto?

No. You of yourself put you in the ghetto.

Good do not seek to live impoverished.

Good do not seek to live in environments that take them from life.

Ghettos did not create themselves. We as humans created ghettos.

And do not come to me with Sociology either because, it is us as Black People that want to be classed in the groups and or, the Socio-Economic Groups White People put you/us in.

Was it not Whites that divide us in the different classes and you went along with the bracket/classes they put you in?

God did not give anyone Black Ghettos to live in.

God did not give anyone for that matter Ghettos to live in.

God did not divide Blacks. We as Blacks divide us, and let others divide us.

You have some that feel the need for power and control however, their control and power they cannot take to hell with them because, NO ONE CAN GO TO HELL AND TELL DEATH HOW TO RUN HELL. Yet, you have people here on Earth that treat you poor as well as, abuse you and their power.

Listen Black People, we are not a powerless race of people yet, we allow others to make us powerless.

Now listen to me carefully.

God did not make God weak on Earth. It is us as humans that weaken God here on Earth. Thus, God cannot come into Earth due to humans desecrating Earth with pure and utter nastiness; evil.

So, now tell me; how can God clean us when, we are unclean, live unclean, marry unclean, pro-

create unclean, worship and praise unclean, pray unclean, die unclean, and more?

IN ORDER TO EAT AND LIVE, YOU SHOULD NOT HAVE TO LIVE THE WAY THOSE THAT DOMINATE AND CONTROL YOU TELL YOU TO LIVE COME ON NOW.

For all the lies the White Race has and have told, they cannot compensate you or life.

For all the killing the White Race and others have done over the years and centuries, they cannot compensate you or life.

For all the diseases and viruses wicked and evil people; diseased men and women design and manufacture here on Earth to harm and kill you, they cannot compensate you or life.

I will not ask how these monsters feel in taking lives.
I will not ask if these monsters have a conscience.

As it is:

BILLIONS CANNOT GET AWAY FROM HELL. THEY MUST; HAVE TO FACE HELL DUE TO SIN.

It's May 04, 2021 and as I was talking to God – Lovey my way. I asked Lovey – God about *SPIRITUAL FORGIVENESS.* I should not have done that. So, as humans that are in the know. For goodness and truth, *truly do not ask God - Lovey about SPIRITUAL FORGIVENESS.* This is wrong and a sin on your part. For me, I had to ask Lovey - God because of the relationship of truth that we have together.

Listen, once Lovey - God severs ties with you or a race, *that severing is indefinite.* You and that Race cannot come back in the fold of God.

I've also told you in other books:

"GOD CANNOT FORGIVE YOU OF SINS DONE UNTO OTHERS. GOD CAN ONLY FORGIVE YOU OF SINS DONE UNTO GOD."

Trust me. *"GOD DO NOT FORGIVE THAT EASILY."*

However, it's not all God forgives. I know this for a fact without doubt thus, many - billions are not of Life. Billions here on Earth cannot be saved.

Now I am going to say this and Lovey; if I am wrong, truly forgive me and correct me because; I truly do not want or need to be wrong, nor do I want or need to mislead anyone.

AS THERE IS PHYSICAL FORGIVENESS, THERE IS/ARE NO SPIRITUAL FORGIVENESS.

<u>*Once the Spirit shed the Flesh all your sins that you have on your Sin Record are deemed as unforgiven.*</u>

Listen, I have never seen or heard of anyone that has died say they forgive the person that has and have hurt them in the living.

Now tell me, who that is dead is going to forgive you of your sins?

Don't look at me. I am not foolish to seek the Domain of Death and go into the Domain and Realm of Death and ask the people you've hurt to forgive you. <u>*WHAT BELONGS TO DEATH BELONGS TO DEATH.*</u>

It's a foolish person that would seek the Realm and Domain of Death for you or anyone.

Yes, many of you are happy for that Physical Forgiveness and, you should be because; you don't have to burn for your Physical Sins. <u>***HOWEVER, YOUR SPIRITUAL SINS ARE ANOTHER STORY. I DO NOT KNOW HOW THIS WORKS SO WHEN GOD LET ME KNOW I WILL LET YOU KNOW.***</u>

I am saying you still have to pay for your Spiritual Debt – Sins. This is because we are both Physical and Spiritual Beings thus the cost of 1 sin is 24 000 x 48 000 = 1 152 000 000.

Yes, the value of 1 sin is 1 billion one hundred and fifty two million years in hell, and this value do not include the days, months, and years you've committed that one sin for.

I fully and truly do not know how Spiritual Forgiveness work if any. Meaning, because we are Physical and Spiritual Beings, I do not know if forgiveness goes both ways for us here on Earth. That knowledge has not been revealed to me by Lovey. Hopefully in due time Lovey will let me know so that I can let you know.

Further, I do not know how this works with Lovey either. So, say forgiveness works both ways. Many are still locked out of Lovey's Domain because; <u>LOVEY TRULY DO NOT HAVE TO FORGIVE YOU OF YOUR SPIRITUAL SINS DONE HERE ON EARTH.</u> And we see this with; <u>BABYLON - THE CHILDREN AND PEOPLE OF BABYLON AND NOW, THE WHITE RACE - THE CHILDREN AND PEOPLE OF SATAN - DEATH.</u>

And though I sound contradictory, I do not mean to be. Still hold this to be true; "<u>GOD CANNOT FORGIVE YOU OF SINS DONE UNTO OTHERS. GOD CAN ONLY FORGIVE SINS DONE UNTO GOD.</u>" And many God do not forgive.

God hath nothing to do with Babylon. The god and gods of Babylon is truly not Lovey and God.

Death is also different for the Children and People of Babylon.

Babylon hath no ties with Life - Lovey and God and now, <u>THE WHITE RACE.</u>

THE WHITE RACE HATH NO TIES WITH LOVEY AND GOD. THE WHITE RACE IS AND ARE LOCKED OUT OF LIFE – THE REALM AND KINGDOM OF GOD.

And like I said in other books. *NOT ALL BLACKS FALL UNDER THE BLACK BANNER OF LIFE. SOME BLACKS ARE WHITE THEREFORE, THEY FALL UNDER THE WHITE BANNER OF DEATH. Therefore, ABSOLUTELY NO ONE CAN TAKE COLOUR OF SKIN TO GOD BECAUSE; "THE COLOUR OF SKIN REPRESENT THE DIFFERENT DEATHS. BLACK SKIN REPRESENT PHYSICAL DEATH – THE DEATH ANGEL THAT HAND YOUR SPIRIT OVER TO FINAL DEATH WHO IS WHITE.*

It is Black Death that read your record for you and tell you how much time you must spend in hell from my knowledge. And Lovey, if I am wrong; please forgive me but, this is how I truly know it to be.

FINAL DEATH IS WHITE THEREFORE, ALL EVIL SPIRITS DIE AS WHITE DRESSED IN WHITE. Thus, many tell you about possession but truly do not know what possession is. Evil cannot possess anyone just like that. And I am going to leave it there because you truly do not know about Generational Curses and or, Sins.

You truly do not know about how people sell their souls here on Earth for Profit – Money, Fame, Control, Dominion, Theft, Rape, all out death, and more.

There are many ways for humans to lose their soul. It is you/us as humans that truly don't know the ways.

So, know for a fact without doubt that people do have evil spirits in them. Thus, the Physical is separated from the Spiritual.

Earth is not the domain of the Spiritual and the Spiritual is not the domain of the Physical even though the spirit and flesh share the same host – our body. And I hope I have not confused you in this way. If I have, think Earth and God and how the two are separated for clarity.

And yes, I will not make this book too long because I am all talked out for now.

This morning; well, it's still morning but; earlier, I was also thinking about Marcus Mosiah Garvey and his efforts in helping Black People in America go back to Africa. For some. *BLACK TO AFRICA.*

He was seeking a better way for Black Americans and they; Black Americans failed him because they did set him up.

Now I ask Lovey. With all that Black Americans has and have done to this man; *CAN ANY BLACK PERSON IN AMERICA COMPENSATE YOU*

LOVEY FOR WHAT YOU TRIED TO DO FOR THEM?

Are they even worthy?

Meaning, *ARE BLACK AMERICANS EVEN WORTHY OF YOU LOVEY?*

No Lovey, I am keeping it full hundred with you when it comes to my line of questions because, it is you that I come to for all. I do listen and did listen. And, you know what I am talking about so truly smile. *I NEED LOVEY THAT IS ALL I GOT TO SAY.*

Now Lovey let me ask you this. *DO(ES) BLACK AMERICANS TRULY WANT TO GO BACK TO AFRICA?*

Now, forgive me for this Lovey. But, *is it wise on your part to allow Black Americans to return to Africa given THEIR BRAINWASHED EDUCATION, MENTALITY, THEIR BETTER THAN EVERYONE ATTITUDE, THE WAY THEY SELL OUT SELF AND THEIR BLACK OWN, AND MORE?*

Forgive me once again Lovey, but; *is it wise on Mother Africa's part to allow Black Americans to return to her and live in her given Black Americans brainwashed education, mentality,* their better than everyone attitude, the way they sell out self and their Black Own, and more?

Yes, you can go there Lovey because; JAMAICANS ARE TRULY NO BETTER. Hence, MANY JAMAICAN RASTAS PRAISE AND WORSHIP SELASSIE A KNOWN BABYLONIAN.

Yes, Selassie a dem gad because; DI RASTAS AND OR, RASTAS TRULY DO NOT KNOW THE TRUTH THEREFORE, THEY CANNOT SPEAK THE TRUTH. THEY CAN ONLY LIE AND LIVE IN LIES. THE LIES THEY'VE ACCEPTED TO BE THE TRUTH HENCE, THEY WORSHIP DEATH AND ARE DEATH – THE SPLITTING IMAGE OF BLACK DEATH – THE DEATH ANGEL INSOFAR AS, THEIR SKIN COLOUR AND HAIR, AND THEY TRULY DON'T KNOW IT. So, when anyone look at a Male or Female Rasta, they are literally seeing Physical Death. The Death Angel period.

Well, they know it now. Therefore, wen dem a bun Babylon. Dem a bun self also. They dug pits for Babylon, and it's them that are falling in the same pits they dug for Babylon.

When Rastas bun Babylon they are truly burning self because, they worship and praise a known Babylonian. *A man period.*

Yes, dem bun battyman but dem a battyman tu. A man dem worship an sey a dem gad. So, now tell me Lovey. WHO ARE THE TRUE FISHES – BATTYMAN OF THIS EARTH. Nuh dem?

Aye sa. A life yaah Lovey. A life.

Now I have lost my train of thought. So, until later Lovey.

Michelle

In all honesty, I am truly tired and fed up of life here on Earth and the way things are. We treat each other poorly, hate each other, do all manner of things to hurt each other, and I am literally fed up. Yes, it's not my life by the crap of shit that we do to each other daily affect us.

Yes, everyone have a right to live their life the way they want to, but why is it for the Black Race; us as Black People this cannot be?

Why is it that our rights and freedom have to be taken away?

What is so wrong with being Black that we cannot live a decent life here on Earth?

What is so wrong with being Black that our rights and freedom must be taken from us by the different races?

And yes, I am going to go there Lovey but; what is so wrong with us as a Race and People that you Lovey have to deny us the right to live free, good, clean, wholesome, positive, and more here on Earth?

Yes, I am fed up thus, I want to leave you now. I can't write anymore. I truly need a vacation from you and all that is happening globally.

Yes, to me, you have failed me. Things are not right away with you. Listen Lovey, I cannot keep praying for me and my prayers are going absolutely nowhere with you. Now tell me, what is wrong with me that when I talk to you and pray to you about me, I get no positive results?

Why is it that I am barred from having a good and true life with you?

I cannot live on disappointment with you therefore for me, and with me, everything is truly wrong about you.

Why should I continue to hurt?
Why should you continue to neglect me?

Shit, why the hell should I continue with you knowing that you cannot give me my needs and wants in that way?

Yes, spoilt me but, I truly do not see progress – positive progress for me here on Earth in that way, and it is sad. Yes, I am having a bad morning and I am so over Lulu.com. I truly want and need to cancel them hence, I truly do not know why I listened to the Woman of Zion and kept true to this platform.

I am so done now because, I have too much heartache with this platform. No Lovey, why does everything with me have to be so damned hard?

Is it this way with you?

Well yes because, all is not what they seem.

I don't know because life is too damned hard for me on some days.

Yes, I need my world and life to be perfect but, what is perfection here on Earth to You and Mother Earth?

I truly don't even want to go there because I was asking you about Black Americans and, yesterday and it seems; never mind. But Lovey, with all that Marcus Mosiah Garvey did to bring Black People back to Africa; why did Blacks turn

Marcus Mosiah Garvey down by setting him up to fail?

We talk about freedom and injustice but Lovey, _ARE WE AS BLACK PEOPLE NOT UNFAIR AND UNJUST TO SELF AND EACH OTHER?_

ARE WE NOT UNFAIR AND UNJUST TO YOU LOVEY?

How can we say we want better and when better come, we turn better down?

How can we say we want better and sabotage our own future?

We did not want better for self then.

I know you are there in some way, and you too have felt the pain and anger of Black People. So now tell me, _WHY DO WE AS BLACKS CONTINUALLY FAIL SELF AND YOU?_

Right now, I am failing you because how I want and need things to be with these books they are not. So, you know what, I am truly going to leave them. On this day, I truly cannot be bothered because I have more heartache than joy with these books. I did try. Now, I have to truly do for myself. This door and avenue I am truly closing for me and you. Stress is truly not a part of my good and true world, and this platform is truly stressing me out, and I truly loathe and hate this platform now.

I need truth not lies, and this platform is truly not my truth but a lie, heartache and problem, just all out false in that way on this day to me.

I will forever say; *THERE IS NO TRUTH IN LIES, AND I CANNOT LIVE A LIFE OF LIES WITH THESE BOOKS ANYMORE.*

I did try but, it's time for me to take a well needed rest from writing these books and just live my life good and clean.

Yes, we've come a long way Lovey, but I am tired of the stress, heartache, and pain. I have not gained in life in my view, and I am going to leave it at that.

No one can walk in your shoes Lovey and eventually talking with you, and walking with you, and not getting any where people do leave. In a way, I am leaving. I need to do me, and for me. I cannot do for you anymore because in full truth Lovey, I TRULY DO NOT SEE A BRIGHTER DAY, AND A BETTER WAY WITH YOU ON THIS DAY.

Maybe I am not the one to lead Blacks where they need to go, and before I die a painful death of disappointment, it's best if I take a break from you good and true. No, I don't need you vacationing with me. I just want and need to walk by myself, do the things I need to do to make me truly happy because, I've told you in some of these books; you truly do not make me happy.

Can Energy and You Lovey be truly happy?

Is there true and lasting happiness in Energy and You Lovey?

Continuing on with Black Americans Lovey, <u>CAN YOU EVEN TRUST THEM?</u>

Yes, everyone I went there.

How can you March for freedom when you of yourself do not know what freedom or true freedom is?

Are we not all caged in someway here on Earth Lovey, given the State of Earth, and who rules Earth?

Today, I don't want to care not even care about You Lovey.

Yes, I need my life day in and day out to be truly positive yet, do you see the condition I am living in?

I am caged in my own world of true doubt on different days with you Lovey and this is truly not good. Maybe I question too much, and you are fed up.

Maybe I know too much, and you are fed up.

Whichever the case Lovey, I need freedom and a free spirit to be truly happy and fulfilled in life.

Right now, I truly do not feel fulfilled in life at all.

Yes, it's a negative day for me. I hold on to things in life that truly do not have true meaning to me with you and you with me if that makes any sense. Thus, I am going to ask you this Lovey.

Is your life meaningful?

What is the meaning of your life, and why do you choose to leave me stranded here on Earth?

Meaning, if your life had true meaning and true worth; value, how come mine; my life here on Earth hath no meaning and true worth; value with you?

Can my life even be valued with you Lovey?

What is value to You Life Wise?
What is truth to You Life Wise?

Like I said, it's a negative day for me because I've put so much effort in these books to be disappointed in Lulu more than big time. Why did I listen to the Woman of Zion Lovey when she too have and has failed me in life all around?

Now, does the <u>*SPIRITUAL REALM WITH YOU*</u> <u>*LOVEY HATH VALUE IN ANY WAY?*</u>

If You valued life there with you, how come you cannot value my life here on Earth with you?

Am I even with you period?
Are you with me period?

Yes, I know I have all the answers to life. You showed me the formulas to life. Lovey, there are so many formulas that I could not comprehend them, nor can I remember the formulas.

So yes, but no. No, meaning, I need to comprehend your language fully and truly. And, stop making me forget because <u>*LIFE IS TRULY NOT*</u> <u>*AN OPEN BOOK WITH YOU AT TIMES.*</u>

Yes, you are there for me, but I need more. What that more is is a true, clean, and good vacation where I can just lounge around and do nothing but walk, eat fruits, swim in the sea, eat roast breadfruit, and just be the good and true me that I want and need to be.

Aye Lovey. I just want to be truly lazy for a day or two where I get breakfast, lunch, dinner, and all my snacks in bed. Yes, the body massage too but unfortunately, I cannot get my heart's desire in this way on this day.

Bummer, yes, I know, but it's my reality and truth on this day and every day.

Now Lovey truly tell me. <u>*Do you look at Black People*</u> <u>*globally?*</u>

If you do. From the beginning until now. No, not from the beginning because Creation did not fail you. Procreation failed you – are nothing but pure evil to the way we are living here on Earth. But Lovey, <u>*from the beginning of pro-creation until*</u> <u>*now including tomorrow, ARE YOU ASHAMED*</u> <u>*OF BLACK PEOPLE?*</u>

Are you ashamed of what we've become, what we do, how we are living, how we've become corrupt, how we treat each other, how we are so accepting of every and anything, how we've accepted Death as our Lord and Saviour even God, how we kill each other, how we are so divided, and more?

I know the life Blacks are living globally is not what you ordained for us so now tell me: <u>WHAT WENT WRONG?</u>

Yes, I know the answer because many of us too licky licky, red yie, cummungin, dungcya, and more.

Lovey, but why though?

Further, what went wrong in Africa for Africans to not be telling the truth?

Yes, I know the answer to that hence, I know the answer to slavery; why Blacks were enslaved. But Lovey, why can't we change our dirty linen of clothing?

You see the way I complain to you and tell you everything. <u>WHY CAN'T WE RETURN TO THIS WAY WHERE WE TELL YOU EVERYTHING LOVEY?</u>

Are you that bad that <u>YOU'VE BECOME A DEAD BEAT DAD; FATHER AND MOTHER?</u>

Yes, things take time with you, but you do answer in your time. Not all but you do answer. The things we know to be the truth, you leave alone because you know we know but Lovey, <u>WHY DID</u>

WE AS BLACK PEOPLE ABANDON TRUTH TO BE VICTIMS OF OUR OWN STUPIDITY?

All you've done to save us righteously we neglect. Many are looking for Jesus to save them. Now let me ask you this; CAN THE DEAD COME BACK TO LIFE AND HAVE FLESH?

No Lovey. I know how the spirit works but, isn't it a foolish man that thinks the dead can gain back their flesh in that way and walk amongst man?

Once the Spirit shed the Flesh, is the Flesh not gone forever ever Lovey?

So, why are humans believing in the Myth of Jesus?

Why are humans thinking you would save them, when not all here on Earth belong to Life; You Lovey?

Thus, humans do live by and in lies Lovey. We also live by and in false hope too.

At times I feel as you are my false hope to the way I see Earth running.

People lie, politicians lie, and more.

I don't know but I do because I am looking for a good, true, clean and positive escape for myself where I do not have to return to the land I am in once I make that final move with you Lovey but, to the way things are going, I truly doubt you and your ability in moving me safely from the land I am in without death and harm coming to me.

You know White People and some Black People truly do not like the truth. We claim but truly do nothing constructive to help ourselves collectively in a positive way so that we can move forward and build Black Positively.

Lovey, there is absolutely nothing wrong in supporting your true Black Own. We as Black People just need to get beyond the barriers that hinder us as a Race and People.

And I am going to end this book here. I don't, truly don't want or need to get so much into it. I need rest from you and writing Lovey, and I am going to do just that.

Yes, it's sad to see what we've become but, it's the choice billions make. Yes, it's not easy staying true to life Lovey given the way some people live, are so evil and get away with it, flaunt what they have, look down on some, but it's them. I cannot look at these things because, I truly do not want or need to live the sleezy way.

I need my life to be pure and void of all ills and wrongs come on now. So no, I cannot wait until 2032. I need all to end now, but I realize our people are not in the land and lands you need us to be in. So Lovey, if the SOUTHERN LANDS OF AFRICA IS WHERE YOU NEED US – OUR GOOD AND TRUE CHILDREN AND PEOPLE IN, THEN TRULY MAKE A GOOD AND TRUE

<u>WAY FOR US TO MIGRATE THERE, AND BE TRULY HAPPY AND PROSPEROUS THERE.</u>

<u>Our prosperity Lovey should truly benefit and help the people of the Southern Lands of Africa come on now.</u>

No showing off but, true help and true thanks Lovey come on now.

How can we redeem ourselves with you if we truly do not have charity – good and true goodness for our good and true Black Own. No Lovey, we cannot support evil Blacks because evil should not be around us.

I truly do not need bondage for our good and true own thus, I bug you for truth and goodness Lovey even when I feel I am not worthy of your goodness and truth at times.

No Lovey, at times I feel as if I am not truthful enough, nor am I truly blessed.

So now Lovey. How do we truly organize this so that our good and true own can escape the Judgement of Earth because you of yourself know that Mother Earth is going to burn. Therefore, the Southern Lands of Africa need to know who they let into their domain?

I truly do not need conflict or war and strife Lovey therefore, <u>I NEED YOU TO TRULY MAKE A BETTER WAY FOR US, THE GOOD AND TRUE THAT WILL NOW SEEK TO LEAVE THE LAND</u>

<u>AND LANDS WE ARE LIVING IN IN A GOOD
AND TRUE WAY COME ON NOW.</u>

I need You Lovey and Mother Earth to be help me make a good and true way for our people. We need the Exodus Lovey come on now. <u>Therefore, those who are not of Life that will now want to flock to the Southern Lands of Africa, PLEASE MAKE ABSOLUTELY NO WAY FOR THEM. LET THESE PEOPLE WHO ARE NOT OF LIFE GET ABSOLUTELY NO ACCESS OR WAY EVER TO THE SOUTHERN LANDS OF AFRICA.</u>

We need to build good and true Lovey not faulty come on now.

Mother Earth and Lovey what is going on?

Evil People are killing us slowly here on Earth come on now.

<u>GOD IS LOVE</u> by Popcaan & Beres Hammond

Gad, di iniquity of the White Race caane done!!!!

Lovey and Mother Earth, what I am seeing from my dream world. Dear God, <u>the genocide worldwide that the White Race get away with, and are going to get away with people Lovey</u> to what I see. Many humans globally cannot see because, they do not have eyes to see before hand like I do.

Mother Earth and God, how do we stop the White Race of Wickedness and Evil here on Earth?

Human Life hath no worth apart from Death when it comes to the White Race. Now, humans are going to further ban dem belly.

Lovey and Mother Earth how come?

How come?
How come?

People if you've not held your family and told them you truly love them, truly hold them now. Tell them you truly love them because, <u>HELL IS GOING TO COME DOWN TO EARTH. Allelujah, Allelujah the INIQUITIES OF THE AMORITES IS NOT YET FULL OR DONE to what I see via my dream world.</u>

<u>If you have no savings in God, truly OPEN A SAVINGS AND CHEQUING ACCOUNT WITH GOD.</u>

Evil is going to kill more.

Wow

It's May 7, 2021 and what I saw this morning, I don't know if I can give a full account of my dream.

The dream had to do with a Small Missile that looked like a Rocket that was fired into the sky. Apparently, there was an issue with a Missile/Rocket in the Sky. The Missile like Rocket was to help fix the issue, but it did not.

No, I am jumping the dream. I was walking with this White Lady. Her child was in the hospital and I was walking with her to the hospital. When we got there; the hospital, the report the nurse had on her child, was wrong. The nurse that was looking after her child lied, and I got upset. The mother got upset too so I said, *"I am going to report the nurse because she was lying."*

Oh God I can't go on. *Allelujah, mi belly Laade Gad tu di evil of the White Race and the LIES THEY IN THE MEDICAL FIELD TELL DAILY.*

Lovey, YOU CANNOT HAVE ANY MERCY NOR, CAN YOU MOTHER EARTH HAVE ANY MERCY FOR THE DOCTORS AND FAMILIES OF NURSES AND DOCTORS INCLUDING, SCIENTISTS WHO LIE AND DESIGN TO KILL – TAKE THE LIFE OF PEOPLE HERE ON EARTH FOR PROFIT, AND THE PURPOSE OF DEATH; THEIR WARPED BELIEFS.

Hell cannot go easy on these people. Therefore, their spiritual fire should match their sins when it comes to burning them. So, if their sins cannot be numbered, then; the fire that consumes them in hell should be as hot as their unnumbered sins. And Lovey, truly forgive me for this because to what I see dream wise, DO THESE PEOPLE NOT HAVE A CONSCIENCE?

Do they value anything at all Lovey?

Do they not think of their spiritual life?

Do they not think of the pain they are causing others?

Do they not think of Hell; their hell in Hell?

Mother Earth what say you here on Earth to what I see?

CAN YOU AS MOTHER; MOTHER EARTH FORGIVE HUMANS FOR THE ILLS THEY DO IN YOU DAY IN AND DAY OUT?

CAN YOU AS MOTHER; MOTHER EARTH FORGIVE HUMANS FOR USING YOUR RESOURCES TO KILL DAY IN AND DAY OUT?

MOTHER; MOTHER EARTH, HOW DO YOU COPE WITH HUMANS – WICKED AND EVIL PEOPLE IN YOU DAY IN AND DAY OUT?

HOW DO YOU STAY SANE MOTHER EARTH?

To what I see, mi haffi ole mi belly.

Mama, di wickedness of evil caane dun inna yu?

Lovey, how do you fully and truly shut the WHITE RACE OF LIARS, DECEIVERS, AND MURDERERS DOWN?

I am getting weak right now just thinking of my dream.

There are doctors and nurses that know the TRUTH OF THEIR COVID 19 LIE but; rest assured for all who keep their mouth shut, and watch people get sicker and die, I know hell awaits them patiently.

For all who know the truth and keep their mouth shut whilst they watch people get sicker and die Lovey, let every sin of those who die and get sick fall on everyone that know the truth and shut their mouth. Let Hell and Death including the Demons of Hell have no mercy on them. Thus, the Sins of the Sick and those who have died Globally, every disease that maim and kill, every virus that maim and kill, every weapon that maim and kill, every bullet that maim and kill, every nuclear weapon that maim and kill, and more must fall on these people (scientists and, doctor that know the truth and shut their mouth, every nurse that know the truth and shut their mouth, every manufacturer and employee of the designers and manufacturers of nuclear weapons, viruses, diseases, bullets, guns, chemicals, and more) – be added to their Sin Record thus, adding move time to their time in hell. This I petition You Lovey, Mother Earth, and Death for. I cannot have mercy for the wicked and evil; heartless of Earth, the Spiritual Realm, and Beyond Lovey come on now.

And Lovey, it matters not the year and century or whether the person is dead; in the Graves of Men. None must escape their judgement.

No Lovey, the wicked and evil cannot go free come on now. If I am wrong, say I am wrong therefore, I have to do that which is right and just. You and I both know that; _ALL WHO HAVE THEIR NAME IN THE BOOK OF DEATH CANNOT AND WILL NEVER EVER ESCAPE HELL._ Therefore, _Death must now adhere to my desire of what is written._

This vaccine; Covid 19 vaccine plus, what I saw in my dream Lovey. HELL MUST STAND AGAINST ALL WHO DEVELOP TO KILL, AND FURTHER INFECT PEOPLE GLOBALLY.

Lovey and Mother Earth, I know neither of you in that way have anything to do with Hell, but I TRULY AND HONESTLY NEED THE BOTH OF YOU TO STAND AGAINST THE WHITE RACE HERE ON EARTH, AND LET DEATH AND HELL HAVE THEIR WAY WITH THEM; THE WHITE RACE.

No pity or mercy must be given to the WHITE RACE AND ALL WHO FALL UNDER THE WHITE BANNER OF DEATH.

The White Race Mother Earth and Lovey neither of you can continue to protect. _YOU MOTHER EARTH HAVE TO AND MUST PROTECT YOU FROM WHAT I SEE IN MY DREAM BECAUSE, NOT EVEN YOU IS/ARE SAFE. Allelujah_

Glory

Dear God have mercy on my soul.

Truly have mercy on me and protect me and the saved from that which is to come. We need you to truly protect us Lovey and God.

Back to my dream.

I cannot remember if it was when I was in the hospital that I saw this White Man dressed in a white lab coat and or, white doctor's jacket. In his hand he had this not vial, or test tube. Think *clear and or, transparent Stash Tube.* He had a green liquid in the tube that was ¾ of the tube. Meaning, the Stash Tube was ¾'s FULL.

No one saw him with this tube because the White Lady from the hospital was no longer with me.

Now I was outside and that was when I saw the Small Missile like Rocket.

After seeing the Small Missile like Rocket and all that I explained above, I saw this huge plane. 3 airplanes were attached to each other. Think in the line of a Super Jumbo Jet with the first plane having a Beluga shape. See with the Small Missile like Rocket not working, they had to send up people into space. 2 Male Babylonians went into space, and they brought back something from the Small Missile Rocket back with them. I said to one of the guys *I thought this was going to take 10 days.* He said no and kept walking. I started a conversation with one of them, and we were having fun talking but his comrade was not receptive of me. He did not like me laughing and talking with this comrade. Leaving me by myself now the two men was at the complex they worked for and one said something about, "ONE RACE HAVING CONTROL." I wanted to chime in and say something to the comrade that was not receptive of me, but I did not get to tell him, "ONE RACE CANNOT HAVE CONTROL."

After that, I was with Nicole Kidman, and Meghan Markle. It looked like we were in a airport. I said something to Nicole

Kidman, and she said something to me about not having PIZZA for her child to eat. She was referring to me petitioning Mother Earth to withhold her goodness from wicked and evil people including, the lands they live in here on Earth. She needed me to ensure her children had food to eat in all of this – that which I petition God and Mother Earth for food wise.

I cannot analyze this dream because I truly do not know if that makes any sense. All I know is:

"WHITE PEOPLE HAVE SOME KIND OF CHEMICAL AGENT THAT THEY ARE GOING TO UNLEASH IN THE AIR."

SO, FOOD IS GOING TO BE THE NEXT TARGET FOR THE WHITE RACE OF MURDERERS THAT LIVE TO KILL.

Insofar as, Water please be watchful.

THEREFORE, YOU WERE TOLD IN, "GOD IS LOVE" by Popcaan and Beres Hammond to "PROTECT YOUR LIFE BECAUSE, EVIL PEOPLE WILL KILL YOU SLOWLY." This is a fact beyond doubt. We see this happening here on Earth with the different diseases and viruses including, weapons, and nuclear weapons that man – humans design and make; manufacture to kill and do kill. Thus, *IT IS THE DEVIL'S CHILDREN AND*

PEOPLE THAT HAVE CONTROL OF EARTH'S RESOURCES – THE ECONOMY OF MEN.

As for Mother Earth, I do not know when she is going to wake up and withdraw her goodness from the different lands of evil. Lands and People who use her resources to take lives. Thus, causing the God of Truth and Life to stay away from her, and out of her.

Humans did cause Earth to Sin because, it's humans that are dirtying her; Earth; Mother Earth day in and day out.

Earth; Mother Earth did let humans cause her shame and disgrace thus, the ills, and wrongs in her that humans do day in and day out.

Listen, I need the wicked and evil to go from Earth. This is my full and good truth. I will not shy from this. For me, _AS LONG AS GOD AND MOTHER EARTH PROTECT ME AND THE GOOD AND TRUE SEEDS GOD HAS AND HAVE GIVEN ME HERE ON EARTH, I AM GOOD TO GO._ However the Demons of Hell and Death devour their wicked and evil own is up to Death, and the Demons of Hell.

I will not interfere with the course of Death in this way because; _BILLIONS TRULY DO NOT BELONG TO GOD. BILLIONS HAVE THEIR OWN GOD, AND BILLIONS DO WORSHIP AND PRAISE DEATH THINKING THEY ARE PRAISING THE TRUE GOD OF LIFE._

KNOW:

NO RELIGION CAN BRING YOU CLOSE TO GOD.

NO RELIGION IS OF GOD.

GOD GAVE NO ONE RELIGION TO CONNECT WITH OR TO HIM OR HER.

GOD IS CLEAN AND GOD TRULY DO NOT GO INTO UNCLEAN PLACES THUS, GOD CANNOT COME INTO EARTH BECAUSE HUMANS MADE SURE THEY LOCKED GOD OUT OF EARTH.

OUR SINS ARE DIRTY.

Lord have mercy to the blackness of sin. Thus, billions truly do not know what their sins look like.

I do not want or need to go to hell therefore, I have to protect my life with God for whom I call Lovey from time to time.

I have to let God be my stay despite me wanting to leave at times.

Listen, the cost of 1 Sin is 1, 152, 000 000. This do(es) not include the days, months, and years you've done that 1 Sin for.

Now think.

1 Earth Day is 24 000 years in Hell. Now, imagine spending 24 000 years in hell and only 1 day is knocked off your Sin Record - Time in Hell.

Do the math.

1 152 000 000 – 1 = 1, 151, 999 999 years.

So, no, I cannot and refuse to go to hell and die spiritually. I have a life with Lovey, and I have to protect this Life with Lovey come on now.

24 000 years and only 1 day is taken off your time in Hell. Hell no, I truly do not love Death or the Demons of Hell in that way come on now.

It is a foolish person that would want to go to hell and burn spiritually.

Woe have mercy on me Lovey because, you are my one and only. Yes, you too Mother Earth and my good and true guides. Therefore, I have to give all of you true thanks because I know, and I have to do all to live good and true come on now.

Now, because there are so many variables in the dream, I truly do not know about India – Asian Lands and if Death is going to consume India – all of Asia again.

Because Nicole Kidman is Australian and an American Citizen, I truly do not know what is going to happen to Australia food and water wise. No, I know. I did dream about Australia, and I did write about it in one of my other books.

As for Meghan Markle. I do not know what is going to happen to the United States of America, Jamaica, and England.

I will not concern myself when it comes to these lands. Lovey, You and Mother Earth have to truly step aside and let Death have their people. Not one of us can interfere. Now I am reminding you Lovey of the time allotted to Death.

Humans did lose 2152 and 2132.

2032 is approaching and we need to gather our good and true own in the land and lands you need us to be in. Therefore, we need to sound the alarm and make a good and true way for our good and true own to find, and get passage to the land and lands we are to be in. We cannot wait until the last minute Lovey come on now.

Lovey.

"TRUTH"

Therefore, absolutely no one can JUDGE THE TRUTH.

Now Lovey tell me. CAN ANYONE JUDGE YOU?

WHAT MAN OR WOMAN CAN JUDGE YOU LOVEY AND GOD?

Now let me ask you this Lovey. If life was precious to humans globally, would they not have good and true people overseeing them?

Would humans not save up some of their goodness and truth in you if they; that person valued their life and the life of their family including, good and true friends?

If humans truly loved their life Lovey, would they have put DEATH ABOVE YOU?

Would humans not know you and, do all to protect their life with you not just spiritually, but physically also?

So now tell me Lovey. *HOW CAN YOU RECEIVE ALL HUMANS WHEN NOT ALL HUMAN – ALL IN HUMANITY BELONG TO YOU?*

Now tell me Lovey. *CAN YOU TAKE FROM DEATH?*

Michelle

<u>*TRUTH IS EVERLASTING LIFE, and God is the truth.*</u>

I know my God is truly not for all therefore, I have to keep God despite the way I write in these books.

It's May 8, 2021, and despite my setbacks in life – God do look out for me.

Did I get the opportunity of a lifetime yesterday by my sister?

Yes, but Jamaica I cannot go into because; <u>*Jamaica is truly dirty.*</u> Yes, I would have loved to go to Jamaica but, <u>*I HAVE TO PROTECT MY LIFE AND PLACE WITH GOD.*</u>

My sister is going home, and she want(s) me to think about coming with her. She will even help to pay for my airline ticket.

Man, just the walk, everything I need food wise, health wise, going to the river, the sea, seeing family, and more is great but, <u>*I CANNOT DISOBEY MY ORDER WITH GOD.*</u>

<u>*GOD HAS FORBIDDEN ME TO GO INTO JAMAICA AND I HAVE TO STAY MY ORDER WITH GOD.*</u> *I cannot accept my sister's offer.*

This is the thing with many Blacks from then until now. Despite God giving them an order to stay their ground, they could not obey God. The Offerings of the Devil was better for them than the

Offerings of God. Thus, you have many in Africa having so many wives that they don't know that they, including their wives, and children are locked out of Life. This is why I tell you, not all African Lands can or will be saved. Many Africans did go against God and are still against God until this day.

I thank my sister for her offer but, <u>I truly cannot disrespect God, nor can I disrespect MY ORDER WITH GOD.</u>

<u>DISOBEDIENCE IS AUTOMATIC DEATH. YOU GO DIRECTLY TO JAIL – HELL ONCE YOUR SPIRIT SHED THE FLESH.</u>

Therefore, when we disobey God, God walk away from us, and take our name out of the BOOK OF LIFE, thus, Death is now your God, and Hell will be your home once your Spirit shed the Flesh. Therefore, it is imperative that you stay your order with God no matter how painful it is.

Right now, many Blacks and Black Lands are hell bound. Thus, I've told you in other books:

"HELL IS FULL OF BLACK PEOPLE, AND RECRUITING MORE."

Thus, life is not over when you are dead – the Spirit shed the Flesh. Those who are of Life and have and has kept the Order of God by having more Good than Sin, then, these people are changed to go up to see God. The rest; all who have more Sin than God have to; must face hell because, Hell is their home. Therefore, the Sin Penalty for billions is high.

I cannot afford to be like Blacks when it comes to God. I have to be obedient.

Many Blacks did lose their place with God due to lies, and many cannot see this. They still believe in Jesus, thinking Jesus is going to come back to Earth and save them. Now I ask you this; <u>WHAT DEATH CAN COME BACK FROM THE DEAD; GRAVE WITH THEIR FLESH AND SAVE YOU FROM HELL?</u>

Many dead are seeking life therefore, it's imperative to know the truth of Life and Death.

God cannot lie to you therefore, if you have no savings with God, God cannot save you.

When you disobey God, God cannot save you. God have to walk away from you.

When you live for Death, God cannot save you. Death must take you and keep you.

If you live to kill, God cannot save you. Death must take you and keep you.

Different Races have different gods yes but; <u>there is only ONE GOD FOR THE BLACK RACE,</u> and none see this or know this.

God cannot be Jesus because; <u>GOD; THE TRUE AND LIVING GOD CANNOT DIE.</u>

God cannot be Jesus because; <u>GOD, THE TRUE AND LIVING GOD IS NOT THE GOD FOR ALL HERE ON EARTH.</u>

God cannot be Jesus because; <u>GOD, THE TRUE AND LIVING GOD CANNOT GO INTO DIRTY PLACES OR HOMES.</u>

God cannot be Jesus because; <u>GOD, THE TRUE AND LIVING GOD CANNOT SAVE THE WICKED AND EVIL; DEATH'S CHILDREN AND PEOPLE THUS, HELL.</u>

So no, <u>*as much as the offer by my sister is lucrative, I cannot accept her offer.*</u> Jamaica is for her because she told me, when she was out there for my gran aunt's funeral, the ground was literally speaking to her. Many of you will not understand the ground speaking to her but I do. More death is coming my family's way. This was and is what the ground was telling her but, she could not comprehend this.

All hath life and Earth, the ground do speak. Think vibration and energy. Listen, Earth do reach out to some, and it's truly hard for me to explain.

Now, this morning I had different dreams, and I am not 100 percent sure if I dreamt Lava flowing. Anyway, my dream world is different as of late and I am so not going to worry about my dream world and dreams. Nor am I going to worry about my dream when it comes to Russia. I cannot worry about the Soul of Billions because, <u>*billions truly cannot be saved literally.*</u>

Dreamt the Reggae Artist Bugle, and he looked a bit older. Listen, I am so not going to get into the dream. All I am going to tell you is, at the end of the dream, I was holding Bugle backway and or, from behind. His back was black and beautiful, and I was kissing his back.

I know what this dream means. Therefore Lovey, <u>I hold your hand, Mother Earth's hand, the hands of all who reside with you Lovey, and truthfully sound the trumpet; ALARM FOR OUR GOOD AND TRUE OWN TO PREPARE, AND DO ALL TO GET OUT OF THE LANDS THEY ARE IN.</u>

You are being warned. It's time to get ready, and it's time to leave. There are no ands, ifs, or buts about this.

<u>PEOPLE GET READY</u> – Curtis Mayfield

I know not all can go back to Africa because, not all have a birthright or ancestral birthright in Africa.

Black People, God did try to help us. It was, and is us that continually believe in the lies and deceit of the White Race, and different races.

None of you realize that the White Race had a job to do, and they did take many of you from life.

Evil devour and kill, it is you as Blacks that refuse to see this as well as, see that Evil – the Children and People of Death is/are killing the lots of you Physically, and Spiritually.

HELL IS GOING TO COME DOWN TO EARTH SO KNOW WHERE YOU STAND WITH GOD IN LIFE.

Lovey and Mother Earth, please open up land space in the Southern Lands of Africa for our good and true own. I know the Southern Lands of Africa is where you need us to be. I will not doubt you because, I know for a fact that not ALL OF AFRICA WILL BE SAVED. We need to be with *you Lovey therefore, we need to be in the region; land and lands you need us to be in.*

<u>*We have to start planting food as well as, secure our good and true waterways.*</u>

Lovey, I need to escape the land I am in and you know, when I am in the land you need me to be in there is absolutely no return for me. I will not come back neither for love, true love, family, money; nothing because I am with you, and I am finally happy and contented. I can plant and bug you even more my way.

The Exodus must now begin Lovey come on now. So yes, <u>I AM SOUNDING THE ALARM BECAUSE THE EXTINCTION OF MAN IS INEVITABLE. THE WHITE RACE OF DEMONS DID DO THEIR JOB THEREFORE, THE GOOD AND TRUE HAVE TO SEPARATE AND SEGRAGATE THEMSELVES FROM DEATH'S WICKED AND EVIL – TRUE OWN</u>.

Now Lovey and Mother Earth. Absolutely no do overs therefore, we must have impenetrable frames, frameworks, and foundations around us continually without end. So, Lovey, if you know people are going to go back to letting evil into their land, home, heart, physical and spiritual DNA, kids, domain, and more; let them not in period. I refuse the old way, and I refuse to mek dunkya Black People or anyone let the wicked and evil back into any domain. Therefore, I need full and true protection for our good and true own.

All access denied to all facets of Evil no matter what that evil is.

Lovey, if I am the only one with you then so be it. I refuse liars and deceivers, cheaters; disobedient children and people who cannot keep the good and true _ORDER OF LIFE._

And Lovey, absolutely no last minute stragglers. Absolutely none allowed. It could be my children. _NO last minute stragglers_ no matter who you/they are.

Lovey, no doing to get either. You know how I loathe people who do to get. So, in all I do, truly thank you Lovey, Mother Earth, and all the good and true guides that are around me.

Michelle

BOOKS WRITTEN BY MICHELLE JEAN 2021

MY TALK JANUARY 2021

MY TALK JANUARY 2021 – BOOK TWO

MINI BOOK

JUST TALKING – THINKING

A LITTLE TALK WITH MOTHER EARTH

I NEED ANSWERS GOD

POETRY MY WAY

THE MIND AND SPIRITUALITY

I NEED ANSWERS GOD – PART TWO

MY NIGHTS

COMING SOON

Open as I am taking a vacation from writing under the Michelle Jean Banner. I need to focus on my novels and in truth, I don't want to, but I have to.

So, if you support me, truly thank you for your support. Never forget, life is not just physical but spiritual therefore, truly protect your life. You are worth it. God is there for you never forget this. You may not think you can be saved from what I write but know: **"I DO NOT MAKE THE FINAL DECISION OF WHO GET INTO THE REALM OF GOD. GOD DOES."** *So, seek the truth of God and let God make a way for. Yes, evil is there but if you are of truth, do truthful things then; worry not. Let God be your guide.*

Michelle